GRASSY STAIRWAYS

Grassy Stairways

John Taylor

*with ten graphite drawings
by Caroline François-Rubino*

MadHat Press
Asheville, North Carolina

MadHat Press
MadHat Incorporated
PO Box 8364, Asheville, NC 28814

Copyright © 2017 John Taylor
Copyright © 2017 Caroline François-Rubino
for the cover and interior illustrations.
All rights reserved.

The Library of Congress has assigned
this edition a Control Number of
2017908409

ISBN 978-1-941196-51-9 (paperback)

Cover art and interior art by Caroline François-Rubino
Cover design by Marc Vincenz
Book design by MadHat Press

www.MadHat-Press.com

First Printing

Table of Contents

Acknowledgments — ix

While thinking of Valery Larbaud — 1

Portholes — 3

At the Edges — 23

The Hinterland — 43

Drink from the Source — 47

Grassy Stairways — 59

Wind — 73

Around Remains of Fire — 87

The Saxifrage — 91

Centers — 95

Between — 101

About the Artist — 108

About the Author — 109

Acknowledgments

The poetic sequences in this book have all stemmed from collaborative projects with the French artist Caroline François-Rubino. "Portholes" and "Drink from the Source" were initially published as bilingual artist's albums in France as *Hublots* (Nantes: L'Œil ébloui, 2016) and *Boire à la source* (Montélimar: Voix d'encre, 2016), both translated into French by Françoise Daviet.

Several poems from the other sequences have been used, alongside an ink drawing or a watercolor painting by Caroline François-Rubino, as "*livres pauvres,*" an international project conceived by Daniel Leuwers. These "poor books" are handmade, by an artist and a poet, in four copies, one of which is kept in a special collection at the Pierre de Ronsard House (Le Prieuré Saint-Cosme) near Tours and the other one used for exhibits. "Poor books" are not sold. They usually consist of a title page, a back page and two inside pages that are illustrated by an image and a poem. And they are each based on the title of an admired book; several poets and artists can thus work on the same title, on the theme that it represents. "The Hinterland" thus refers to Yves Bonnefoy's *L'Arrière-pays,* and "Around Remains of Fire" was written for a "poor book" series based on Bonnefoy's *Les Planches courbes* (The Curved Planks).

Poems from the title sequence, "Grassy Stairways," were similarly used in the "poor book" series *Cahier de verdure* (Notebook of Greenery), the title of one of Philippe Jaccottet's books that I translated and published in *And, Nonetheless: Selected Prose and Poetry 1990–2009* (New York: Chelsea Editions, 2011). The title, "Grassy Stairways," alludes to the narrow stone stairways, overgrown with high grass, that can be found on the levee that runs along the right bank of the Loire River, specifically near the village of Saint-Mathurin-sur-Loire.

The opening poem, "While thinking of Valery Larbaud," was also used in a poor book.

John Taylor

The sequences "Wind," "Centers," and "Between" were used by Caroline François-Rubino and me for *"livres uniques,"* that is, handmade books in a single copy. Our collaborative work was displayed at the Bordeaux Public Library in September 2016. Let me express my gratitude to Sophie Chambard, who organized this exhibit, and to her husband, the poet Claude Chambard, for his hearty moral support and good cheer! More collaborative work—including the artist's many projects with other poets—was shown at the Pau Public Library in April–May 2017.

"The Saxifrage" was written in English and published in French in a special section of the French online journal *Terre à ciel* (December 2015) that was dedicated to the memory of Clara Pop-Dudouit, the daughter of the Romanian Francophone poet Sanda Voïca.

Earlier versions of some of these poems were originally published, bilingually, in the French online journals *Terres de femmes, Paysages écrits,* and *Terre à ciel*; and in Marco Morello's Italian translations, in *Samgha, Il giornacio,* and *L'Ombra delle parole*. One poem from "Portholes" was published on the *Antioch Review* blog, along with the text "Writing on the Train."

While thinking of Valery Larbaud

your name your face fade
again and again

into this landscape
that ever faces you
that ever flees

its perpetual flight
cannot be halted

yet swiftness also
cradles everything
without exception

and you must accept this

Portholes

quick crests
waves in the twilight

lines
scribbled
with water
on water

ever less lit

*

now and then
darker speckled shadows
on the shadow of night

ever less lit

*

cluster of lights
halfway up
whichever shadow
was

*

John Taylor

    cliffs edifices
       resist

   the inevitable
    enveloping

*

  shapes effaced
  night emerges
     words
      blur

    the porthole
is the last remaining form

*

  dark blue night
  welcoming in
   whatever is
      was
   parallel to

*

dust
round the rim

mere certainty

*

what is torn
between night and day

will words mend

*

through the porthole

the porthole of night

*

John Taylor

    fingers imagined
    over the waters

    even when
    grayed from rose
    blued from rose
    bedecked with night

*

    in the soft
    light blue
    light

after night has fled

flecks of night
or flights
of unknown birds

*

through mist

the island
rising
to what
has risen

*

this island
or another

*

bluish
blue
clarity

off to the side

outside

*

John Taylor

    through the porthole
       hazy lines
       of matter

        matter

*

       the haze
    clouds the pane

   over the water
     imagined
     delicacy
     of haze

*

   not far away
  ship sailing away
   another way

*

center
in the porthole

the sun

whitening
at the end
the beginning

*

sometimes the island
the mountain
the seawater
the mist over the seawater
are one

blue
gray
insubstantial

nothing

were it not

*

John Taylor

    darken this side
    so the other side
        retains
         light
        longer

*

        salt
        sand
   beating the pane

    fingernails
scratching the pane

         ago

  nicks negating
  the now outside

*

squaring the circle
of the porthole

ever
between

possibilities

*

from sun
to moon

caught uncaught
by clouds

shimmering
sea
shore

*

John Taylor

the porthole
of memory

rimming
tingeing
the blankness
blue

*

still unseen
unforeseen

*

seawater swelling
midway to
whatever island

in motion matter
blends

outside the porthole

blue gusts

*

rough sea
on that side

on this side
of the porthole

*

never
a sea crossing
without peril

peril
the point
or the passage

*

open the porthole

your hand in the wind
good as any eye
for what must be seen

*

John Taylor

no thoughts
of the end

except this

*

having left
everything

behind

the blue source

*

against sleep
you peer out

the cerulean circle

rimmed
with midnight blue

*

these portholes

this mountain
on which you remember them

gray drizzling
over the slopes
over the sea

*

stowing possibilities
below

the perspective

*

withdrawn
until

surges

the blue whirl

*

John Taylor

encircling what
could coalesce

*

a precise
blur

this passing
present

*

what is given

the shifting
shades of blue
the vertical
the horizontal

the horizon
with its backdrop
of rising
sinking
light

*

was it at dawn
the departure

at dusk

or midday
dolphins
cloudlike streaks
over the waves
the sunlight
subdued
sovereign

*

John Taylor

                voices
              on the deck

              the voices
            you seek to hear
            those of the sea
               the haze
        the shadows on the shadow

          the whitening light

                the blue
                the night

          your ear on the porthole

                    *

              from the deck
                 a vista

              finding words
                 a focus

            what you learned
             from the porthole

                    *

handful of olives
soaked in seawater

like this seawater
soaked in earth and air

sustenance

*

circular rim
unrim

*

standing back

or breath
on the pane

you are facing

*

John Taylor

you knew
new night would
encircle
day breaking

ever less lit

Samos, August 1976–Bessans, August 2014

At the Edges

at the edge
of the blue woods
a clearing
hesitates

now and then
you leave the edge
enter what awaits

    *

this clearing
the only tenable
temporary
certitude

and the crest

    *

John Taylor

smudges smears
tracings
signs

then signature

recognizable ridge

never without hints
slants or shades

the original
structure

the original blue
that seems
substance

the real crevasse
and the imagined heart
of the glacier

*

GRASSY STAIRWAYS

unsure
you ever would have sought
a pane of ice
instead of this prism

the sheen of ink
on slope and stream

     *

John Taylor

constrained
by the blue
enveloping

by the blue
smothering

blue wherever
she couldn't
wonder without

the maternal blue
was an exact shade
a self-cast shadow
then a shroud

at her birth
two rivers
her meandering
melancholy
below a mountain

now taken
into my hands

this other blue
she never knew

*

blue or blue
in its darkness
lightness

shapeless

void of substance

yet in it you seek
the non-void

    *

shifting blues
shifting shadows
in their movement

among the mountains
among the waters

you are also there

you think

or wish

    *

John Taylor

waves before you
and the way back up the cliff

the border

then away
or away

      *

the ending
of the end

the field of all origins
whatever will be
the last space
will flow
into endless
or ending
light
or night

      *

beneath delayed doom

the distant hawk's rise
from chance
from contingency

will sculpt the mountain
into wings
vying with the cloud
for less impermanence

then reduced
into sky
even
the hawk's flight

    *

John Taylor

amid the flow
whatever bends
with the flow

remains firmer
than your firmament

outlasts
your lasting
longing

*

sometimes the forest
thins
the clearing
thickens

left right
up down

the secret wish
for whirl

*

the mountain breaks apart
under the falling snow

here and there vanish

woods paths possibilities

floating mountaintop

but all remains
blue

at heart

you think

from that heart
to its edge

    *

John Taylor

blue streaks
across the light
on the light

sometimes you deemed the blue
night

the white
light

named the white
blankness

but it was not the blankness

    *

it was enough that you turned
the field blue
the trees blue
the hills blue
the path blue
the unclimbable peaks of clouds
blue
from their original blankness

now you must accept
the blue field
the blue trees
the blue hills
the blue path
the unclimbable peaks of blue clouds
in their original blankness

    *

John Taylor

drowning in air
falling through water
burning
blending with the earth
its blue embers

within the unmoving
haze
ever briefer sparks

of your instants

    *

often the field
seemed scribbled
with the blue stubble
of lost learnable words

off the path
in the plains
was the summit

    *

forest shadows
dark clouds
welcome the wounds
sabers of sunlight

whatever spurts forth
after the light
spatters you
you call it impossible

blood

*

unending afternoon
a hill to till

while you are gazing
at the blankness

behind the blue

at the distance
at distance

*

John Taylor

the strict equivalence
cannot be

neither wish
nor need it
otherwise

confined
by ends
beginnings
so you end again
begin again

the vast bay of endings
you linger there
before moving on

as far as possible

still so close

so it was
between form and formlessness
the not quite yet
the blurred cohesion
before division
before definition

you wish to shape

upon its emergence

even after its departure

    *

infinity impermanence
darken
disproportionately

so in your brevity
you seek the dark-rooted
the dark-stemmed
the dark earthly blues

landscapes remembered
imagined

other darknesses
as brief as you

    *

John Taylor

childhood snow
blue snow

pathless
possible

forever vanished
newness

now in rivulets

    *

dark blue mountains
mere clouds

each illusion

the memory
of another illusion

where vanished meadows opened
onto thunderclouds

as unreal
as their reality

ever before
now
and ever after

The Hinterland

Endless Ending Paths

behind the present
beyond
inside

endless mountain
endless

ending paths

while waiting in that room
you follow
each
with your eyes

tunnel bend
or boulder

bringing endings

to distant footsteps
on endless

ending paths

Drink from the Source

Garnets in the Gravel

Well beyond the end of the old trail: a moraine to scale, then these sudden garnets.

*

Garnets in the gravel, water dripping from the glacier's lip.

*

Amid the garnets, searching for the perfect dodecahedron.

*

Having walked around the dried-up lake, but according to the map another one higher up.

*

Raise your eyes: the summit above you unfolds ever upwards, into the blue and the clouds.

*

As glacial water drips on your hands, these garnets in the gravel, again and again.

Obergurgl, July 2004

John Taylor

Willow Stick

Dead willow branch: a hard hiking stick, and the slope increased.

*

Above this alpine pasture an eagle soars out from the cliff; and as I look down, a viper crosses my path.

*

The waterfall inaccessible because of the moraine.

*

("No symbols where none intended.")

*

Enormous chamois-like shadows moving across the high meadows of the Ouille Allegra.

*

Not a soul coming down.

*

John Taylor

Hidden valley below the glacier: water flowing down in fingers, a fertile greenness in the pasture. High up, an eagle flies out from a dark rift that is like a secret passage.

*

Between two meadows, the sunken lane on which we often met the woodcarver, toward sunset. Toward the sunset.

*

Redstart alighting at the base of the village cross.

*

A cloud like a harrow in the air; and the next evening, another cloud-harrow; then continuous rain for days.

*

Deep-blue gentian flowers along a path so high that the last vegetation was ending and we were increasingly surrounded by stone. The stained-glass windows of Chartres.

*

La Dent Parachée: the candelabrum just below the peak has lost most of the eternal snow that had made each candlestick distinct, summer after summer. This candelabrum now a persistent memory.

*

A single upright stone in the meadow across the torrent. No cow or cowherd has ever pushed it down, rolled it over to the bank.

*

Some of the rain seemed to be the very cotton grass that was also sprinkled over the alpine marsh.

*

Of the pulsatilla anemone I wanted to write: "With a score of arms reaching out."

*

Hundreds of jackdaws jolting off the cliff, as if tossed like straw into the wind.

*

The same willow stick: not a divining rod.

*

Words rising in French: *séneçon, circe, nigritelle.*

*

Paradisea liliastrum, the paradise lily: a common mountain flower with a heavenly name.

*

At the end of dusk, when cloud and mountain had so blended that neither could be distinguished. But it was not yet night.

*

Above the fog, Charbonnel Peak and Mount Albaron not so faraway. The illusion of being close to them. Clouds of unknowing below. Humidity like a magnifying glass.

*

A tongue of fog coming down from the Mont Cenis Pass; and I would like this tongue to speak a language.

*

Bridging the rapids: stepping stones, yet well under water by midday when we returned.

*

The tractor's headlights on the highway. The last load of mowed meadow grass. Heading home. 10 p.m. Soup. Alone ever since "the wife" (as he calls her affectionately) died.

*

Roots. This alder torn from the bank by the floodwaters of the Arc, swept downstream and then washed up, upside down, on a distant mudbar.

*

Tiny pale-violet colchicum flowers, as in the French song, constellating a meadow mowed only yesterday. Birth into bloom: the last surviving flowers before the first snow.

*

A flat stone (serpentine) left where we first found and examined it in the meadow. Our marker on the way back.

*

A path visible again, now that the meadow has been mowed. A centuries-old path.

*

A few more yards down the trail and you stop once again, look around. Every single mountain slope, every single perspective up valleys and between peaks, seem changed in significant ways. And have not changed significantly at all, of course.

*

Village in the hollow beneath its church and cemetery, beneath ancient moraines now covered with high grass and larches. Village above the rapids of the Arc.

*

August sunrise. But this time, night has left snow on the summits.

*

Soft larch needles grazing a hand: both unlasting.

*

Chaos of fog and sunset-lit clouds up the Avérole Valley. And
    patches of blue sky as well. Admire, but await a gentler,
    simpler evening.

*

The fog, I think, is moving faster across the green
    mountainside than I thought.

*

Early morning in late August: larch logs burning in every
    fireplace.

*

Drink from the source beneath the boulder, imagining it is
    something else. It is nothing else.

Bessans, August 2008

Grassy Stairways

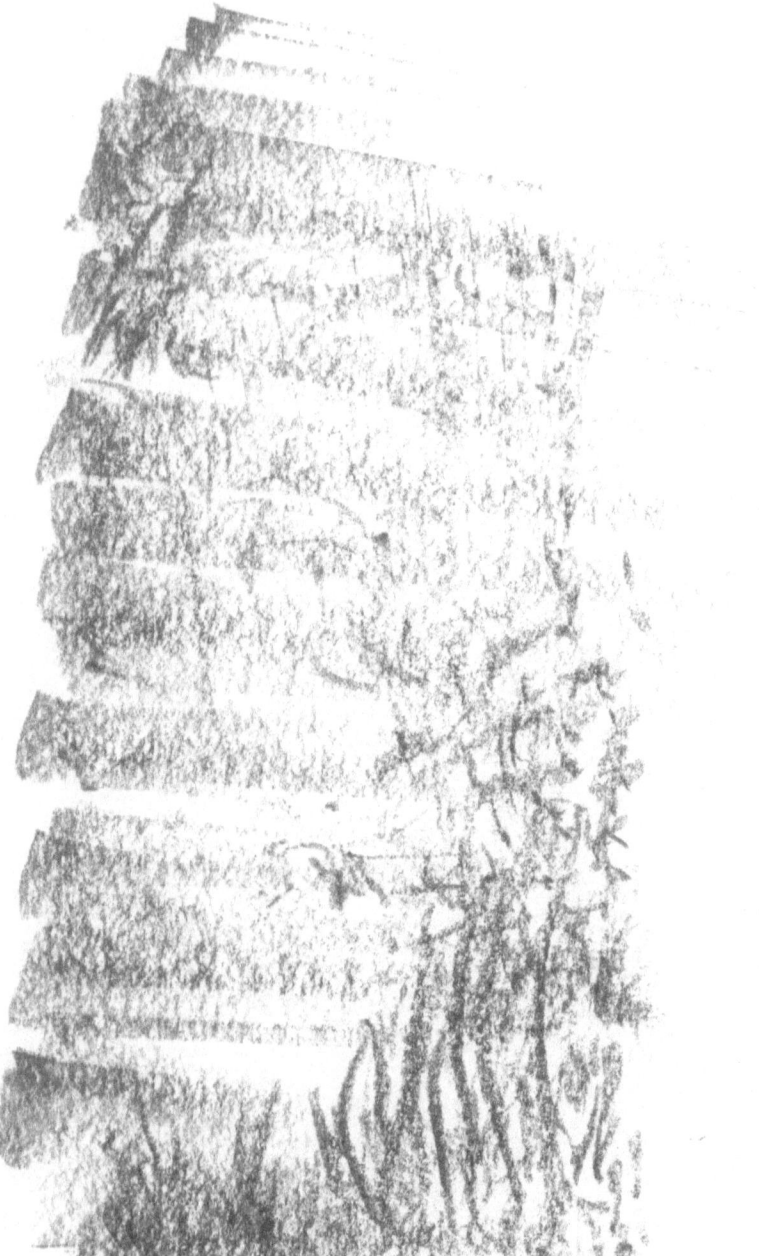

dandelion
lit
midway up
the overgrown path
of steps

midday
for a little longer
than this moment
moving on

    *

John Taylor

what seems to last
the yellowish lichen
higher up

winter spring
in fall
climb again

the sunlight cast
on the first steps
cannot retain you

it dazzles
blurs the right angles
all the lines

    *

unshackling yourself
from no shackles

the memory of them remains

up the stairs
back down
back up

the memory remains
but not in the grass
but not on the stone steps

    *

John Taylor

rising
into the lowly

the high grasses rooted
in the gaps
the high grasses bending
over every step

woolen wings
come down from heaven

you are sheltered
in their yellow warmth
and shadow

you think

*

and sometimes stairs
resist
what grows over them
closes them in
closes them off

climb again

halfway up

to the side
in daylight
that clump of night
sprinkled with pale yellow petals
light and lasting
as snowflakes

John Taylor

||

forget not
the forget-me-nots
the fragile poppies
to the left
of the steps

yet imagine not even
to gently hold

*

you thought the stairs
were going up

they were heading down

through high grass rising
through every space
through every geometry

*

four stair steps only
uncovered by the grass

then impossibility

the only possibility

*

like a stem wandering
across the bottom step

as if not to say farewell

*

the high grass flowering
into seed

snowflakes in the sunlight
in the summer wind

*

John Taylor

steps emerge
at eye level
from the indistinguishable

from the overgrowth

from the chaos of grasses

through which you are
ascending

or

looking back

descending

     *

farther

higher

it seemed clearer

this aliveness we know
scarcer

stone and stone

in sky
no longer stone
nor step

    *

John Taylor

every stair step
cradled in grass

cradled in heaven

in the void

with invisible grass

you still
seek to imagine

*

only thinkable
as step
a first stair step

high stone wall
along a meadow

rung-less
stepladders of grass

stalks broken
seed unspent

*

Grassy Stairways

the stairway seems to turn away
because of the wind blowing
the high grasses
left over from winter

from the onset
illusion and observation

the short spring sprouts
cover nothing
cradle nothing

at the bottom missing rung
where the rule is established

Wind

wind within
this stillness

only you can measure it

    *

you're wide awake
within this day

where the wind
is edged with night

    *

wind
of winter boughs
and cold flames

only their
hollow flickering
motionless swaying
as landmarks now

    *

John Taylor

when everything
bears down

this upshoot of wind
sudden sprout
from no seed

amid the rocks
so far below

*

the wind turns
rushes against you

you are less divided
less often over there
and here

more often
even

one and the same

*

gentle wind
neither in your face
nor behind you

from the side

a barrier
a no-man's land
even this tenderness

between you
and something ahead

that will drift away
in the gentle wind
coming from the side

you think

over there
forever there
only there

never here

    *

John Taylor

it might have been
woman or bird

wind
swirling

mere shape
something
you cannot slow down
sharpen
with your geometry

wind
swirling

from dust
to dust

figments of fancy
you can always refute
but not forget

*

puffs of wind
on your mother's cheek

no longer here
no longer there

each puff
on your cheek

turns your cheek
your eyes

to where the wind
bears everyone to where

here is no longer
there is no longer

    *

John Taylor

after the elms
traces in the air

like branches
like rungs

then nothing
but wind

a ladder leaned
against the sycamore
dwarfed till then

the lowest branch
as out of reach

already in the same
unreachable

windy
nothing

*

the next morning
starker shadow
because of the starker light

outside the circle of darkness
of dimness
of soothing grayness

the brightness is blinding
bodiless
windless now

within is a path

it passes by
your shelter in the shade
of the sycamore

*

John Taylor

for every path
there is wind

from the east
from the west
from the north
from the south

columns of wind-
ladders wind-ropes

wind-steps cut into stone
or muddy trails
leading away

    *

geometries of wind
that become blurs

that show you
lines filling out
into surfaces
shapes

and often
what is vague lineless
blows

across your life
across your eyes
clouds your sight

you accept
these night winds
these day winds

live within
all the gray winds

*

John Taylor

imagine wind
in your cupped palm

holding it there
for instants

instants

you seek to feel again
winds remembered and

none can be felt

again

every wind has blown away
left you at best
with this thought

no breeze
caresses the back of your hand

no feather you can cradle
in your half-open hand

and watch trembling

*

an instant of wind
and windlessness

when you forget its feel
on your lips

when the wind
is on the ridge
the other ridge

      *

this wind
you sense as a burden
on your face

it casts sand
in your eyes
stings bites

blinding you to what
you wish to see

you bear this
wounded desire

not what is

Around Remains of Fire

Grassy Stairways

around remains of fire
charred wood in a circle
we would gather in the shade
of a hedge
of a wooden garage

until one day a boy
smashed his head
against a stone

after that spilt blood
sunlight was veiled
or too bright
shadow often darker
or somehow absent
when it should have soothed

so we left behind fantasies
of fire embers ash
all that was vague and even more remote
yet nearby

—in our hands

water flowing
through a blue landscape
endless hills in our flat farmlands
ageless climbable oaks—

John Taylor

abandoned what had seemed shade
the calm and cool afternoons
during the slow summers of childhood

(the hedge and garage rose
to the north)

for what now appeared the true

sky
through the lofty leafy
limbs of the elm
in the next yard

up to now forbidden

broad daylight like a single swath
through the dense hedges
sheltering us alluring us
and for years thereafter we forgot
we would once again seek shadows
ancient fires vistas from tree houses
water flowing through a blue landscape

The Saxifrage

if only the snake
had been of words alone
as it hid under the stone
and the stone mere paper

but those saxifrages you planted
still lift to the hardened sky
cups of soothing bloom
tiny mouths of song

that split that shatter no rocks
as the poet thought
only sprout among them
rise in summer

like chords

and when the season comes
cover the snake's coldest stone
with their lovely little bowed heads

Centers

the center shifts
while still the center

*

the path leads only in thought
from
and to

*

gazes away
are towards

or at a standstill
at a spot no longer there

or here

*

within
is without

or edge

or edgelessness

*

John Taylor

    thinking here
is thinking there

or nowhere

imaginable

is this state
of statelessness

*

am was
am will be

else
elsewhere
elsewhen
elsehow

you go

*

rivers almost the same
mountains almost the same

the leaf falling
still attached to the twig
of the other tree

*

as if another dust
and ash

*

wind even within
the stillness

*

two centers
or none

shimmering
betweenness

pathless
and possible

Between

what grows
between
we know what it is

*

as you were
as you are

as I was
as I am

what
between
is

*

between you and you
between me and me
between you and me
I wonder
you wonder

*

John Taylor

between
betwixt

sometimes the betwixtness

is comical
and worrisome

*

between here
and there
(between you and me)
the mere thickness
of that word

between
the two
hesitant
impatient
waiting
words

that are the same word

*

the indivisible knows

no inner
betweenness

*

between
two betweens
two borders to cross

then this in-between
shelter
near the next border

*

ever among
ever untangling
strands between

(betwixt)

*

John Taylor

    between evening
  and the night I imagine
     this glaring
      daylight

*

    differences
  ever differences
    'tweening
    twaining

*

  when betweenness
   narrows to nil
I cannot forget the distance
    diminishing

*

from the beginning

betweenness

instead of void
between

*

between
an answer
and a question

between this night and Night
between Night and That Night

*

between no's

is the yes

About the Artist

CAROLINE FRANÇOIS-RUBINO is a French artist who was born in 1960 and currently lives in southwestern France. Along with her philosophically resonant personal work, which is often oriented toward our innermost experiences of landscape, she has published two artist's albums in France in collaboration with John Taylor, *Hublots* (Éditions L'Œil ébloui) and *Boire à la source* (Éditions Voix d'encre). She has worked on joint projects with many French and European poets.

About the Author

JOHN TAYLOR, born in 1952, is an American writer, critic, and translator who has lived in France since 1977. His most recent books of poetry and short prose are *The Apocalypse Tapestries* (Xenos Books), *If Night is Falling* (Bitter Oleander Press), and *The Dark Brightness* (Xenos Books). As a translator, he has won grants and prizes from the National Endowment for the Arts, the Sonia Raiziss Charitable Foundation, and the Academy of American Poets. In 2015, his translation of José-Flore Tappy's poetry (*Sheds*, Bitter Oleander Press) was a finalist for the National Translation Award of the American Literary Translators Association. His recent translations include books by Philippe Jaccottet, Pierre-Albert Jourdan, Pierre Chappuis, Catherine Colomb, Georges Perros, Alfredo de Palchi, and Lorenzo Calogero. His critical essays on European poetry in general and French literature in particular have been published in five volumes at Transaction Publishers, the latest of which is *A Little Tour through European Poetry*.

www.ingramcontent.com/pod-product-compliance
Lightning Source LLC
Chambersburg PA
CBHW020335170426
43200CB00006B/389